The Infant of Prague

How the Child Jesus can help us

by
Glynn MacNiven-Johnston

*All booklets are published thanks to the
generous support of the members of the
Catholic Truth Society*

CATHOLIC TRUTH SOCIETY
PUBLISHERS TO THE HOLY SEE

Contents

With thanks to Mercedes Turu Plaja for advice on all things Spanish.

All rights reserved. First published 2014 by The Incorporated Catholic Truth Society, 40-46 Harleyford Road London SE11 5AY Tel: 020 7640 0042 Fax: 020 7640 0046. © 2014 The Incorporated Catholic Truth Society. Page 22, © Office Central de Lisieux.

ISBN 978 1 78469 004 5

Introduction

It may seem curious that devotion to the Infant of Prague is so strong. Surely we are too sophisticated nowadays to pay attention to a wax statue dressed in odd, frilly clothes? Often the devotion focuses on material needs. Isn't this a bit like praying to win the lottery; just a superstition of the kind modern Catholics should be embarrassed about? But this devotion is shared or at least respected by some very serious people including Pope Emeritus Benedict XVI who crowned the statue when he made an Apostolic Visit to Prague in September 2009. And this is a devotion promoted by the Carmelites. Carmelite spirituality emphasises an intense and direct relationship with Jesus Christ; it has a deep love for Mary and is based on an internal life of contemplative prayer. As the Rule of St Albert says, they are called to live a "life of allegiance to Jesus Christ." This is a spirituality which attracted the highly intellectual Edith Stein, St Teresa Benedicta of the Cross. It is far from being 'frilly'. In the end, too, it is not wrong to ask for our material needs (needs rather than wants). The Lord's Prayer itself tells us to ask for our daily bread. Again we should not forget that material needs for many people means enough to stay alive for that day or enough to feed their children or pay for medicine. These are not frivolous requests. And despite its, to modern eyes, somewhat odd appearance, this is a statue of the Child Jesus. This is not idolatry. Nobody imagines that the statue is alive. It is merely a means of meeting the living Christ.

When Pope Benedict XVI visited the shrine, he said that the image of the Infant of Prague reminds us of "the mystery of the incarnation of the all powerful God who became man" and lived in a family as a child. He prayed in front of the statue for parents, for families, especially those struggling with illness, suffering, infidelity and other crises, entrusting them all to the Infant. He also prayed for all those children who are "neither loved, nor welcomed, nor respected; for those children who 'suffer violence and every form of exploitation." Children, he said, are "the future and hope of humanity" and every person is "a child of God."

The Infant of Prague Statue

The statue now known as The Miraculous Infant of Prague
has been in the Carmelite Church in the Malá Strana district
of Prague since 1628. The statue, only 45cm (just under 18
inches) tall on a 2cm (circa 3/4 inch) base, represents the
Child Jesus. It has a wooden core covered in linen and the
outer part is carved in wax. The Child's left hand is cupped
and his right raised in blessing. The statue itself is modelled
wearing a simple gown but it seems that the statue was
always also dressed in clothes made of fabric.There are
records of other similar statues and the clothes that were
made to honour them, so it appears that clothing statues
was formerly common practice. Although the wax statue
has mid-length wavy hair it also has a blonde wig made
of real hair. Since the mid 1700s the statue has been robed
in elaborate clothes of the style we now associate with the
Infant of Prague. Some of the clothes are in the style of
seventeenth and eighteenth century court dress and they
are all intended to show Christ as universal priest and king.
The set of clothing is formed of a simple undergarment,
a robe, and a mantle with sleeves. There are also lace
cuffs and a ruff which are sometimes separate. The statue
occasionally wears a ring on each of the first two fingers
of his right hand. These were given in 1788 by a noble

family in gratitude for the healing of their daughter. The cupped hand of the Infant is made to hold an orb, of which there are several. There are also three crowns. The crowns do not sit on the statue's head but are suspended above it. The newest of these was donated by Pope Benedict XVI in 2009. The Infant has over seventy different outfits which have been given over the years from many different parts of the world and many of the costumes can be seen in the museum attached to the church. One of the sets was hand sewn by the Habsburg empress Maria Theresa, who had a love for the Infant of Prague even if, as was widely believed, she was not too fond of her Czech subjects. One set of robes given by a Chinese convent is embroidered with prayers for the people of China. There are also clothes given by individuals most notably from the Philippines.

These days the wax of the statue is very fragile, so to prevent further damage the statue is encased in silver up to the waist. The statue is dressed with great reverence by the Carmelite Sisters and the colour of the robes is matched to the Church's year. The annual feast of the Coronation of the Infant Jesus is on the first Sunday of May.

Unexpected Connections

Over the years the Carmelite church of Our Lady of Victory has been much embellished. The interior is now Baroque in style with a great deal of gilding. The statue of the Infant of Prague is set in an elaborate gilt and glass case on the central altar. Above the case is a sunburst with a representation of God the Father and the Holy Spirit and on either side are gilded statues of Our Lady and St Joseph.

The Infant is much loved in Prague even by those who are not believers and for this reason it survived in a country where religious practice almost disappeared during Communist times; though even during the Communist period pilgrims continued to come from all over the world. There are also unexpected connections. Antoine de Saint-Exupéry was familiar with the devotion to the Infant of Prague and it is said to have influenced him in writing *The Little Prince*. Pilgrims still visit in large numbers seeking help, feeling able to approach a God who loves us so much he became a child for us.

The Origins of the Statue

Surprisingly perhaps, the Infant of Prague is not from Prague. Its origin is Spanish. Legend says that the statue came into being in this way: in the Middle Ages, in Spain between Cordoba and Seville, there was a famous monastery but, as it was in the path of the conquering Moors, it had been attacked and damaged many times so that eventually only four monks remained in the semi-ruined buildings. One of these monks was called Fray José de la Santa Casa (Brother Joseph of the Holy House). One day he was cleaning the floor and a small boy was watching him. "You are cleaning the floor very well," said the boy.

"Thank you," said, Fray José. "Can you say the Hail Mary for me?" asked the child. Obligingly Fray José began reciting the Hail Mary and when he arrived at the line, *"et benedictus fructus ventris tui"* (and blessed is the fruit of thy womb) the child said "that is who I am" and vanished from sight. "Come back!" called Fray José. "I will," said a voice, "but you must make an exact model of me." Fray José went to see the prior and explained. The prior gave him some wax and a knife and he began to try to produce a likeness of what he had seen. Eventually he managed to produce an exact likeness. After a while the Child Jesus appeared to Fray José again, this time accompanied by angels. Fray José was very happy to see that the likeness he had made was true and, soon after, he died and was taken to heaven by the angels who accompanied the Child.

The legend also claims that Fray José appeared to the prior a little later telling him that the statue was not for the monastery but that someone would come for it and take it to Prague.

Whether or not we want to take this story literally, it is known that the statue was brought to Prague by a Spanish noblewoman named Doña María Isabel Maximiliana Manrique de Mendoza y Lara y Briceño (c.1538-1608). She was given the statue by her parents, in 1558, as a wedding present when she married a Bohemian nobleman, Vratislav z Pernštejn, one of the richest men of his time. One story says that Doña María's mother, Doña Isabel, was the one who found the statue at the monastery as Fray José had foretold, but the Lobkovic family, Doña María's descendants, insist that the statue was given to Doña Isabel by St Teresa of Avila who was a friend of hers.

Bohemia

Vratislav z Pernštejn was the middle son of a Protestant Moravian - Bohemian family who, aged thirteen, was sent to the Viennese court of the Holy Roman Emperor Ferdinand I. There he was educated with the emperor's nephew Maximilian (later Maximilian II). Vratislav and Maximilian remained close. In 1548 Maximilian married his first cousin, María, the daughter of the Spanish king, Charles V. María Manrique was one of the Empress María's ladies in waiting. By this time Vratislav had become Catholic, along with his elder brother. Vratislav and María had twenty children, seven of whom, two sons and five daughters, survived into adulthood, so with the worry of so many children, Doña María probably had recourse to the Infant Jesus often. The statue also reminded her of her homeland. It is said she never got used to the cold in Bohemia. Vratislav was wealthy but he also had a lavish lifestyle and he soon had to begin selling off some of his property to support it. After Vratislav drowned in a shipwreck in the Danube in 1582, María had financial problems as well as the difficulties of finding suitable husbands for her five daughters. We may suppose that she turned for help to Christ who had a special love for widows, and turned to him using the image of the Infant. She did in fact manage to find husbands for them all, with the marriage of her middle daughter, Polyxena, considered the most propitious despite the fact the groom was almost thirty years his bride's senior and a rather singular man who, at one point, apparently became a Rosicrucian (the Rosicrucians were an obscure secret society of uncertain origin and purpose). Vilém z Rožmberka came from one of the most important families in the empire and he had been married three times before; all of the marriages were childless. Polyxena was given the statue of the Child Jesus as a wedding present.

A late pregnancy

Perhaps María felt that since her own marriage had been so blessed with children through her devotion to the Child Jesus, he might be able to help Polyxena entering into a marriage with a man who had had no children despite having had three wives. This marriage, like Vilém's previous three, remained childless. After five years, Vilém died leaving Polyxena extremely rich. She went to live in Roudnice, in one of the castles she now owned. It seemed she would not remarry, but eleven years later in 1603 she married Zdeněk Vojtěch Popel z Lobkovic who was the head of the Catholic Party and Supreme Chancellor of Bohemia. At the time of their marriage Zdeněk and Polyxena were both in their thirties and it began to look as if this marriage too would be childless. Polyxena, like her mother, surely turned to the Infant Jesus in her suffering. Finally, though she was forty-two, Polyxena had her only child, a son called Václav Eusebius. Zdeněk, like Polyxena, was a committed and devout Catholic and the couple were involved in several projects including having a Capuchin monastery built on their estate. In 1628, widowed for a second time, Polyxena presented the small statue (which she called her most prized possession) to the Carmelite church in Prague, telling the friars they would never want while they had the Infant Jesus to take care of them. She must have experienced the Infant's material provision during the time, after the death of her father, when her own family were struggling financially.

The Carmelites in Prague

The Carmelite church, built around 1613, had been a Lutheran church called Holy Trinity, serving the German speaking community until 1620 when, after the Battle of the White Mountain and the victory of the Catholic forces, it was handed over to the Discalced Carmelites by Emperor Ferdinand II. In 1624 the church was consecrated to Our Lady of Victory and St Anthony. When Emperor Ferdinand asked the Carmelites to take over the running of the church, he had promised them financial support, but up to the time they were given the statue they had received nothing. The emperor suddenly made good his promise as soon as the friars received the statue.

To begin with the statue was placed in the oratory of the monastery for private devotion and as a help for the novices, but after a time it was moved into the church itself. Soon parishioners and others began to pray in front of the Christ Child and miracles began to be reported. Our Lady of Victory became a place of pilgrimage for the sick, the suffering and especially for those who desired children.

A widely quoted early text says:

"All who approach the miraculous statue and pray here with confidence receive assistance in danger, consolation in sorrow, aid in poverty, comfort in anxiety, light in spiritual darkness, streams of grace in dryness of soul, health in sickness and hope in despair. ...No colic is so painful, no fever so violent, no malady so dangerous, no peril so great, no tumour so malignant, no insanity so raving, no complaint so irritating, no assaults of Satan so furious, no pestilence so infectious, no swelling so serious, as not to be dispelled or cured by this Blessed Child. The Holy Infant puts an end to enmities, frees prisoners, saves those who are condemned to death, and blesses childless parents with off-spring. In short he has become all to all."

Fr Cyril and the Christ Child

In the same year as the statue was presented to the Carmelites, Fr Cyril of the Mother of God was sent to Prague. Born Nicholas Schockwilerg in 1590 in

Luxembourg, he entered the Carmel at a young age and was ordained priest in 1624. In Prague he developed a great devotion to the Infant.

Two years later however, in 1630, the Carmelites had to flee as the city was over-run by Protestant armies from Saxony. Mercenaries occupied the monastery; the church was looted and vandalised. Everything of value was taken. Apparently this did not include the statue of the Infant. It was tossed behind the altar. After the Treaty of Prague in 1635, the Carmelites began to return. Fr Cyril was sent back in 1637 and it was he who found the broken statue in the rubble. The blue robe the Infant was wearing caught his eye. The statue's hands were broken off. With the prior's permission he placed the statue in the oratory once more. One night Fr Cyril was alone praying in front of the statue when he heard a child's voice say, "Have mercy on me and I will have mercy on you; give me back my hands and I will give you peace. The more you honour me, the more I will bless you."

Fr Cyril was amazed but he did want to do as the Child asked him. The prior was less enthusiastic as the church had no money even for food let alone any spare to pay for the repair of a statue. There are various versions of what happened next, but most give this story. First, an old man, whom everyone had thought very poor, suddenly donated a large sum of money to the church. It was enough to buy a new statue so that is what the prior did, rather than try to repair the broken, dirty, old one. As soon as the new statue was placed on the altar, a heavy candlestick fell over and smashed it.

Fr Cyril still hoped that the old statue would be repaired, but there was no money left. Then, one night he was called from prayer as a lady had asked to see him. In the darkened church, a woman was waiting quietly and when he approached her she handed him a purse full of money telling him to use it so that the monastery did not suffer. She then left. All his life Fr Cyril remained convinced that this lady was the Virgin Mary herself. Still, though, Fr Cyril had no say over what happened to the money. It was used to rebuild the church. Bit by bit the church and its treasures were restored. The small statue remained broken and ignored.

Once again while in prayer, Fr Cyril heard the Child's voice tell him, "Place me at the entrance to the sacristy and you will find the one who will have mercy on me." This is what happened. Someone seeing the broken statue offered to pay for the repairs and a young artist was found who did the work. It is further said the young man was so moved when the statue was whole again that he left without asking for payment.

Fr Cyril remained at the monastery and devoted to the Child until his death in 1675 aged eighty-five. His body was placed in the catacombs beneath the church.

Lost in War, Recovered in Peace

During more fighting triggered by the Thirty Years' War, the Protestant Swedish army occupied the left bank of the Vltava River and the Carmelite prior persuaded the Swedish General von Konigsmarck to set up a patrol to protect the church and monastery. Injured Swedish soldiers were treated in the monastery and another of the Swedish generals, Prince Karl Gustaf, who later became King Karl (Charles) X. Gustaf visited the Infant and left a donation of thirty ducats. The people who lived in the Malá Strana area brought their belongings for safe keeping and some even sheltered there. With the Peace of Westphalia, the war finally ended.

The Prague Carmelites discovered that, as the Child had said to Fr Cyril, the more they honoured the Infant, the more he helped them. When devotion to the Infant flourished, so too did the monastery. The fame of the Infant Jesus began to spread, first as a helper of the childless, and copies of the statue began to appear in other countries. He was also invoked by those in material need; especially the poor to whom this can be a life and death issue.

In 1648 the Archbishop of Prague, Ernst Adalbert, Cardinal von Harrach, gave ecclesiastical approval to the devotion to the Miraculous Infant of Prague. He consecrated the chapel on 3rd May 1648. In 1655 the Infant was crowned and devotion was then declared to be to the Infant King.

Miracles continued to be reported and many were recorded by one of the priors, Fr Emericus of St Stephen who collected the testimonies and miraculous events (including the protection of the city from the plague), publishing, in 1749, a book detailing them.

In the eighteenth century Jan Schlansovsky, a sculptor, carved a mould of the Infant of Prague. From this, hundreds of copies of the statue were made and sent to countries throughout the world.

In 1784 the Prague Carmel was closed by decree of Emperor Joseph II and the church and shrine passed to the administration of the Knights of Malta. But, since love of the Christ Child was part of Carmelite spirituality, devotion to the Infant of Prague was promoted and copies of the statue taken all over the world with the Carmelite communities. Devotion to the Infant of Prague continued at the shrine also and even during the Communist period pilgrims came from all over the world. In 1993 the Cardinal Archbishop of Prague, Miloslav Vlk requested that the Carmelites return and there are currently both priests and nuns who care for the shrine.

Miracles

Many miracles received through the Infant of Prague have been reported. One of the early ones concerns Hraběnka (Countess) Alžběta Kolowrat z Libštejn who was sent the statue of the Infant when she went blind during an illness. Her sight was miraculously restored and she returned to health. However, the countess was a relative of the Lobkovic family and presumably believed she had some claim to the statue so after her healing she did not return it to the shrine. A little later she decided to leave Prague and take the statue with her. It is said that her horses would not move until the Infant was removed from the carriage. The countess repented and returned the statue; she and her family became great supporters and patrons of the Prague Carmel. During the seventeenth century there was an outbreak of plague in Bohemia and the disease was ravaging the country. One night the prior saw a glow from the chapel and afraid that the votive candles had set fire to the building he rushed in to check. Instead he saw the orb the Infant was holding, slowly turning and glowing. Seven small figures knelt before the glowing globe. As the Prior looked the vision faded and the next day the plague was halted.

There have been more modern miracles too. Dr José Rodríguez Sanjuan wrote about the miraculous healing of his infant son Nicolas, in Puerto Rico in 1985. The baby needed cardiopulmonary resuscitation and lay comatose and on the edge of death for seven days. On the seventh day someone left a small statue of the Infant of Prague at the hospital reception asking that it be given to the family. On receiving it, and having nothing to lose, Dr Rodríguez placed the statue next to the child's cot and went to the chapel to pray. After a while a nurse came rushing in to the chapel telling him that Nicholas had woken and begun to breathe independently. He developed normally and has continued to have a normal life.

Another witness is an Indian woman who was paralysed in an accident and confined to bed. She had a dream about the Infant of Prague and woke up knowing she could be healed. She began a novena to the Infant and as she prayed she noticed that feeling was gradually returning to her body. After a few weeks she was able to move normally. In the 1990s she fulfilled her wish to visit the shrine in Prague having saved for fifty years to be able to do so.

The Infant of Prague in the Philippines

In 1521 Ferdinand Magellan, a Portuguese in the service of Spain, discovered a group of islands which he claimed for Spain and which were later named the Philippines after Philip II of Spain. Magellan set up his base on Cebu. The chaplain of the expedition, Fr Pedro Valderma, began preaching the gospel to the inhabitants and many accepted Christianity. Among them was Queen Humamay who, after her baptism, took the name Juana.

Magellan gave her a statue of the Infant of Prague to celebrate her baptism. This copy, like the first one brought to Ireland, was made in Belgium. Unfortunately Magellan was killed in a battle with a neighbouring tribe and his men returned to Spain. In 1565 another expedition arrived but the people of Cebu, afraid that this was retribution for Magellan's death, responded with violence. They were routed by heavy artillery and fled to the hills. As the Spaniards searched the ruins, a soldier, Juan Camus, discovered the statue in a wooden box. The people had hidden it fearing the Spaniards were going to ask for it back. The painted wooden statue was undamaged and it is that same image which is in the Basilica Minore del Santo Niño today. The basilica was built on the site where the statue was found. This statue has survived various catastrophes. It was undamaged when the basilica was bombed in World War II and survived an earthquake in 2013. The Infant, or Santo Niño de Cebu as it is known, is considered to be the oldest Christian relic in the Philippines. The Santo Niño is celebrated by Filipinos with feasts, parades and a special dance called the Sinulog. The dancers take two steps forward and one back imitating the flow of a river. Dancers accompany the carriage carrying the statue as it passes through the streets. The Sinulog festival takes place in Cebu on the third Sunday of January.

The Infant of Prague in Ireland

Devotion to the Infant of Prague, though popular, is quite recent to Ireland, a statue having been brought from Belgium to the Carmelite Monastery in Loughrea in 1890.

Ireland was a poor country and many people had pressing financial concerns. A custom arose for newly married couples to be given a statue of the Infant with a coin, usually a sixpence, underneath, to ensure there would always be money in the home. In more modern times in Ireland, a country with high rainfall, brides asked the Infant to send a sunny day for their weddings and to make sure, the statue was put outside. These practices might seem silly to more sophisticated people but they are folk practices based on a familiarity with the love of Christ for us.

Devotion to the Child Jesus

Even in the light of all this history and testimony, we may still be unsure about the nature of this particular devotion. Why should we pray to Jesus represented as a young child, an infant even, rather than the grown man who went willingly to the cross for us?

There can be no doubt that this devotion is a long-standing one. From the beginning Christians have been helped by the fact that Jesus had a childhood. He was conceived, born and grew up in a family. The Gospels speak of the events surrounding his birth and although they give only an outline of his childhood and youth there is enough to show that its happening was important. The festivals of the church - Christmas, Candlemas etc. - also underlined this. It is important for us to know that God became man and experienced everything, every part of the life we experience. As the nineteenth century Protestant hymn writer, Mrs Cecil Frances Alexander, wrote in *Once in Royal David's City*:

"For he is our childhood's pattern;
Day by day, like us he grew;
He was little, weak and helpless,
Tears and smiles like us he knew;
And he feeleth for our sadness,
And he shareth in our gladness."

St Thérèse of Lisieux and other sisters with the Infant of Prague statue.

Saints of the Christ Child

God himself became vulnerable for us. His love for us is such that he became weaker than us. We are called to be children of God, but God himself entrusts himself to our care. We receive him in the Eucharist. We receive him in our hearts. We are helped to understand the love God has for us by this manifestation of the all-powerful God as a helpless child. It helps us to be open to love and be loved by him. In human terms, even the stoniest hearts can be moved by the joyful love expressed by a small child. It is a love without conditions. St Jerome, who was notoriously grumpy, had a vision of the Nativity while he was staying in a cave in Bethlehem - perhaps the very cave where Christ was born - and he was so moved that in his vision he spoke to the Child, asking what he could give to him. He made various suggestions, but the Christ Child pointed out that all these things had been made by him and belonged to him already. Eventually Jerome asked again if there was anything that he could give him. The Child said he could give him his sins, so he, Christ, could take them away. God in his great love for us became a child so that we could understand that he loves us unconditionally as children do. The statues of the Child Jesus are there to remind us of this.

Throughout the ages there have been saints to whom Christ has appeared as a Child. Famously there is St Anthony and especially St Teresa of Avila who was instrumental in

introducing this devotion into the Carmelites. One story
says that Teresa was about to go upstairs when she met a
small boy. "What's your name?" he asked. She replied with
her name in religion - Teresa de Jesús - Teresa of Jesus.
What's your name?" she asked in return. "I am Jesus of
Teresa" he answered. This encounter affected her so deeply
that whenever she founded a new convent she brought a
statue of the Child Jesus and encouraged the devotion.

This custom led to another Teresa in another Carmel
producing the famous Little Way. Thérèse of Lisieux,
whose name in religion was Thérèse de l'Enfant-Jésus
(Teresa of the Child Jesus), was devoted to the Child Jesus,
and as novice mistress encouraged devotion to the Infant
of Prague. She believed that people at the time emphasised
fear of God too much and wanted to show that nobody
should be afraid of a God who became a child for us.

Many other people have agreed with her, especially those
whose country had been conquered or whose people had
been oppressed, or who had been introduced to a rigid or
militaristic form of Christianity. The Jesuits, for example,
bringing Christianity to South America, found that the
indigenous people there immediately connected with the
Christ Child and were much more willing to listen. It was a
faith born not of conquest but of an understanding of love.

*"Majesty made itself small so that those who held it
could endure it."* - St Ephrem the Syrian

Other Famous Images of the Child Jesus

Santo Bambino di Aracoeli

The small chubby statue of the Santo Bambino di Aracoeli (on the Capitoline hill in Rome) is said to have been carved in the fifteenth century by a Franciscan friar, from olive wood taken from a tree in the Garden of Gethsemane. The face of the statue was, they say, painted by angels while the friar slept. Many miracles have been attributed to the Santo Bambino especially regarding illness. The statue is still taken to the very sick and dying. On the 25th of every month, oil is taken from the lamp that burns in front of the Santo Bambino and put into small bottles to be distributed to the sick.

At Christmas during midnight Mass, the Bambino is moved from his private chapel and placed on a throne in front of the high altar where he remains for the Christmas season. Many children come to visit at this time and sing songs and recite poems.

In fact the current statue is a copy as the original was stolen in the 1990s and has not been recovered. However, the miracles have continued: it is not the statue itself which is miraculous but the connection to the Child Jesus.

El Santo Niño de Atocha

This devotion originated in Atocha, Spain when the Moors invaded and took many Christians prisoners. The prisoners had no food and their relatives were told that only children under twelve years old would be allowed to visit the prison. Those prisoners and their families who had no young children were in despair. The families prayed in front of a statue of the Virgin and Child, Our Lady of Atocha. Soon a small boy began appearing at the prison bringing food for the men who had no small children of their own. The child was dressed in a robe and a large floppy hat and had the pilgrim shells from Santiago de Compostela. He brought a basket of food and a container of water, neither of which ran out until they were no longer needed. People began to suspect that the child might be Christ himself, a belief borne out when they saw that the shoes on the statue of the Child were worn out. This devotion passed to Mexico where it became very popular and where there is now a major shrine. El Santo Niño de Atocha is often invoked for prisoners and for healing, especially the healing of children. Pilgrims to his shrines sometimes leave children's shoes there.

The Little King of Grace

Marguerite du Saint Sacrament (Margaret of the Blessed Sacrament) was a Carmelite at Beaune in France. She entered the convent aged only eleven in 1630 but she was a remarkable person who had been caring for the sick since she was five years old. Devotion to the Child Jesus was encouraged at the Beaune Carmel by Cardinal de de Bérulle who had encountered it at the Carmel in Spain. Sr Margaret entered deeply into this devotion and received a private revelation of the chaplet of the Holy Child. At that time also, Anne of Austria, the wife of the French King Louis XIII, had no son after almost twenty years of marriage. Sr Margaret prayed to the Infant Jesus and in a revelation was told that the queen would have a son.

A Norman baron, Gaston de Renty, heard about this and visited the Carmel to meet Sr Margaret. She introduced him to devotion to the Infant and he had a statue of the Infant made and sent it to her as a gift. This statue, now called Le Petit Roi de Grâce (the Little King of Grace) can be visited in the monastery which bears his name. When Sr Margaret died in 1648 documentation was immediately collected in order to take forward her cause. Testimonies were given including Queen Anne of Austria's, and the documentation was taken to Rome. But the process came to a halt when the bishop who had the documentation died suddenly and the papers were lost. The French Revolution put an end to everything until 1865 when the documents were finally found. Sr Margaret was declared venerable in 1905.

Devotions

Act of consecration to the Holy Child Jesus

O Divine Child Jesus, only-begotten Son of the Father, you are the true light that enlightens everyone coming into this world. It is through you that I am, it is through you that all things have been made, and without you nothing would be. It is therefore just that I devote myself to you without reserve.

In gratitude for all the love with which you love me, I devote to you all the love my heart is capable of. I ardently desire to love you still more, to offer you a heart less unworthy of you. Accept this ardent desire, O Divine Child Jesus, and kindly bless it.

You have suffered for us in order that we might one day deserve to be associated with your eternal happiness. I want to unite my sufferings to yours, so that you may give them merit and they may be sanctified. As you have been weeping for me, because of my sins, help me by your grace to weep for them myself.

I also devote to you all my joys. May I only have the ambition and the will to seek those pleasing to your service, by the practice of the virtues taught in the mysteries of your Divine Childhood. I beg you to help me by your grace to acquire the gentleness, the humility, the childlike simplicity, the filial confidence and the perfect obedience you showed.

Or:

O sweet Child Jesus, who didst manifest thy power and mercy through a little waxen figure of thyself in Prague, I wish to proclaim thy royal dominion over my soul and body.

Deign, O Little King of Heaven, to watch over my work, bless my enterprises both temporal and spiritual, to dispel my cares, to sanctify my joys, to alleviate my sufferings.

Grant me pardon for all the offences I have committed against thee, for I know that thou art good and merciful to the penitent sinner. Thine I am. Thine I wish to remain, loving and adoring thee, Little King of Heaven. Take possession of my whole being; do with me whatever thou wilt. I desire, like St Thérèse, thy Little Flower of Carmel, to be thy playmate. Make me love thee more and more, that one day I may see thy sweet face smiling from thy throne in Heaven.

Prayers by Fr Cyril of the Mother of God OCD

Jesus, you decided to become a child, and I am coming to you full of trust. I believe that your attentive love forestalls all my needs. Even more than the intercession of your Holy Mother, you can meet my necessities, spiritual as well as material, if I pray according to your holy will. I love you with all my heart, all my strength.

I beg your pardon, if my weakness makes me sin. I repeat with the Gospel "Lord, if you want you can heal me." I leave you to decide how and when. I am ready to accept suffering, if this is your will, but help me not to become hardened to it, rather to bear fruit. Help me to be a faithful servant and for your sake, holy Child, to love my neighbour as myself. Almighty Child, unceasingly I pray you to support me in my necessities of the present moment. Grant me the grace to remain in you, to be possessed and to possess you entirely, with your parents, Mary and Joseph, in the eternal praise of your heavenly servants.

O Infant Jesus, I run to you,
begging you through your Holy Mother
to save me in this need
(*you may name it here*),
for I truly and firmly believe
that your divinity can defend me.
Full of trust I hope in you
to obtain your holy grace.
I love you with all my heart,
I am painfully sorry for my sins
and on my knees I beg you,
O Little Jesus, to free me from them.

My resolution is to improve
and never more to offend you.
Therefore, I offer myself to you,
ready to suffer everything for you
and to serve you faithfully.
I will love my neighbour as myself
from my heart for the love of you.
O Little Jesus, I adore you,
O Mighty Child, I implore you,
save me in this need
(*you can mention it here*),
that I may enjoy you eternally,
with Mary and Joseph see you
and with all the angels adore you.
Amen.

Another version:

Jesus, unto thee I flee,
Through thy mother praying thee
In my need to succour me.
Truly, I believe of thee
God thou art, with strength to shield me.
Full of trust I hope of thee
Thou thy grace wilt give to me.
All my heart I give to thee
Therefore, do my sins repent me;
From them breaking, I beseech thee

Jesus, from their bonds to free me.
Firm my purpose is to mend me;
Never more will I offend thee.
Wholly unto thee I give me
Patiently to suffer for thee;
Thee to serve eternally.
And my neighbour like to me
I will love, for love of thee.
Little Jesus, I beseech thee
In my need to succour me,
That with Joseph and Mary
And the angels, I may thee
Once enjoy eternally. Amen.

Prayer by Pope Benedict XVI

O my Lord Jesus,
we gaze on you as a baby
and believe that you are the Son of God,
who became man
in the womb of the Virgin Mary,
through the working of the Holy Spirit.
Just as at Bethlehem,
we too, with Mary, Joseph,
the angels and the shepherds,
adore you and acknowledge you
as our only Saviour.

You became poor
to enrich us with your poverty.
Grant that we may never forget the poor
and all those who suffer.
Protect our families,
bless all the children of the world,
and grant that the love you brought us
may always reign amongst us
and lead us to a happier life.
Grant, O Jesus, that all
may recognise the truth of your birth,
so that they may know
that you came to bring
to the whole human family
light, joy and peace.
You who live and reign
with God the Father
in the unity of the Holy Spirit,
one God, for ever and ever. Amen.

Prayer of St Thérèse of Lisieux

O Little Infant Jesus, my only treasure, I abandon myself to thy every wish. I seek no other joy than that of calling forth thy sweet smile. Grant me the graces and the virtues of thy Holy Childhood, so that on the day of my birth into heaven the angels and saints may recognise me as thy little spouse.

Morning Offering to the Holy Child Jesus

O Sweet Infant Jesus
I offer you my will that you strengthen it
My mind that you inspire it
My memory that you fill it
My wishes and desires that you cleanse them.
I sacrifice to you
My intentions that you guide them
All my actions that you make them holy.
All I am and have is yours.
Your love for me is my hope and trust.
Hear me and grant that I never leave you.
Amen.

Chaplet of the Holy Child

Venerable Sister Margaret of the Blessed Sacrament, (1619-1648) a Sister of the Beaune Carmel in France, received a private revelation of Our Lord in which she was given a chaplet in honour of his childhood.

The chaplet, known as the Little Crown, consists of fifteen beads and a medal of the Child Jesus.

On the medal say, "Divine Infant Jesus, I adore thy cross, and I accept all the crosses thou wilt be pleased to send me. Adorable Trinity, I offer thee for the glory of the Holy Name of God all the adorations of the Sacred Heart of the Holy Infant Jesus."

The first three beads are in honour of the Holy Family: Jesus, Mary, and Joseph.

On each of these beads say "And the Word was made flesh and dwelt amongst us"

followed by the Our Father.

The other twelve beads are in honour of the Holy Childhood of Christ.

On each of them say "And the Word was made flesh and dwelt amongst us,"

followed by the Hail Mary.

At the end of the chaplet say "Holy Infant Jesus, bless and protect us."

During each Hail Mary meditate on the mysteries of Jesus's childhood:

1. The incarnation
2. Life in Mary's womb
3. Birth in Bethlehem
4. Adoration of the Shepherds
5. Circumcision
6. Adoration of the Magi
7. Presentation in the Temple
8. Flight into Egypt
9. Life in Egypt
10. Return to Nazareth

11. Hidden life in Nazareth
12. The twelve-year-old Jesus in the Temple

In the revelations to Venerable Margaret, the Divine Infant promised to those who meditated on these mysteries the gifts of simplicity, innocence, purity of heart, humility and obedience.

Prayer to the Child Jesus

Child Jesus, I come to you.
Child Jesus, look at me.
Child Jesus, listen to me.
Child Jesus, I have faith in you.

Make my heart gentle and humble
Like yours.
Pure and innocent
Like yours.
Obedient and confident
Like yours.
Generous and patient
Like yours.

Detach me from everything that keeps me far from you
Let me live the joys and trials of this life
In simplicity and perseverance
Like you and for you
And may I enter at last into the glory of heaven
With you. Amen.

"Prayer in Affliction" to the Infant of Prague

O dearest Jesus, tenderly loving us, thy greatest joy is to dwell among men, and to bestow thy blessing upon us! Though I am not worthy that thou shouldst behold me with love, I feel myself drawn to thee, O dear Infant Jesus, because thou dost gladly pardon me and exercise thy almighty power over me. So many, who turned with confidence to thee, have received graces and had their petitions granted. Behold me, in spirit I kneel before thy miraculous image on thy altar in Prague, and lay open my heart to thee, with its prayers, petitions and hopes. My greatest need in particular - (*mention your intentions here*) - I enclose it in thy loving heart.

Govern me, and do with me and mine, according to thy holy will, for I know that in thy divine wisdom and love thou wilt ordain everything for the best. Almighty, gracious Infant Jesus, do not withdraw thy hand from us, but protect and bless us forever. I pray thee, sweetest Infant, in the name of thy Blessed Mother Mary who cared for thee with such tenderness, and by the great reverence with which St Joseph carried thee in his arms, comfort me that I may bless and thank thee forever with all my heart. Amen.

Act of Thanksgiving to the Infant Jesus

O most gracious Infant Jesus, prostrate before thee, I offer thee most fervent thanks for the blessings thou hast bestowed upon me. I praise thy mercy and confess that thou alone art my God, my helper, and my protector. Henceforth, my entire confidence shall be placed in thee, everywhere will I proclaim thy mercy and generosity. May devotion to thy holy infancy enter more and more into the hearts of all Christians, and may all who experience thy assistance persevere in returning unceasing gratitude to thy most holy infancy; to which be praise and glory for all eternity. Amen.

A simple prayer to the Infant Jesus

Little Jesus, thank you for bringing us safely through this day (this night).Help us to bring your smile of friendship, your love, the Good News and your healing into the lives of those people we meet and those in need.

Infant Jesus, shower us with your blessings that we may worship you in peace, and be permanently dedicated to the service of your kingdom. Amen.

Prayer of a sick person

O merciful Infant Jesus, I know of your miraculous deeds for the sick; how many diseases you cured during your life on earth, and how many venerators of your miraculous image ascribe to you their recovery and deliverance from most painful and hopeless maladies.

I know that a sinner like me has no right to ask for favours but in view of the innumerable graces and the miraculous cures granted even to sinners through the veneration of your holy infancy, particularly in the miraculous statue of Prague, I exclaim with the greatest assurance:

O most loving, most merciful Infant Jesus, you can cure me if you will! Do not hesitate, O heavenly physician, if it be your will that I recover from this present illness; extend your most holy hands, and by your power take away all pain and infirmity.

If, however, you in your inscrutable wisdom have determined otherwise, then restore my soul to perfect health, fill me with heavenly consolation and blessing, that I may be like you, O Jesus, in my sufferings, and may your providence enfold me until you, at the death of my body, bestow on me eternal life.

Prayer for a sick person

O Holy Child Jesus, lord of life and death, I implore you to cure (*name the person*) who is so dear to my heart.

He/she is in great suffering, racked with pain, and can find no relief except in you, in whom he/she puts his/her hope. Relieve him/her, O heavenly doctor, free him/her from suffering and give him/her perfect health, if that be your divine will and for the good of his/her soul. Amen.

Our Father; Hail Mary; Glory Be to the Father.

Novenas

Urgent Novena

Say once an hour for nine hours on one single day

O Jesus, who has said ask and you shall receive, seek and you shall find, knock and it shall be opened to you, through the intercession of Mary, thy most holy Mother, I knock, I seek and I ask that my prayer may be granted.

(*Mention your intentions here*)

O Jesus, who has said all that you ask of the Father in my name, he will grant you, through the intercession of Mary, thy most holy Mother, I humbly and urgently ask thy Father in thy Name, that my prayer be granted.

(*Mention your intentions here*)

O Jesus, who has said "Heaven and Earth shall pass away, but my word shall not pass away", through the intercession of Mary, thy most holy Mother, I feel confident that my prayer will be granted.

(*Mention your intentions here*)

Other Novenas

These novenas are to be said once a day for nine days. They can be said over any nine days but especially from 17th to 25th December.

Novena to the Child Jesus

O Miraculous Child Jesus, the heart of a child is kind and generous. Your heart is infinitely kind, infinitely generous. May your tender heart incline to pity and grant the grace I now implore (*mention it here*).

Take away my despair and the burden of my trials and misfortune. Send me consolation and help me, I beg you. I turn to you with childlike confidence and thank you for hearing my prayer. Amen.

Longer Novena

Day 1

O sweet Child Jesus, here at your feet is a soul that, conscious of its nothingness turns to you, who are all. I have so much need of your help. Look on me O Jesus, with love since you are all powerful, help me in my poverty.

R/ Our Father...Hail Mary...Glory Be...

By your Divine Infancy, O Jesus, grant the grace that I now ask (*express it*) if it is according to your will and for my true good. Do not look upon my unworthiness but show me your infinite mercy.

Day 2

O splendour of the heavenly Father, in whose face shines the light of divinity. I adore you profoundly and I confess you as the true Son of the living God. I offer you, O Lord, the humble homage of all my being. Grant that I may never separate myself from you. *R*/

Day 3

O Holy Child Jesus, in gazing upon your countenance, from which comes the most beautiful of smiles, I am filled with trust. Yes, I hope in your goodness. O Jesus, smile on me and on those dear to me. I praise your infinite mercy. *R*/

Day 4

O Child Jesus, whose head is adorned with a crown, I accept you as my absolute sovereign, I no longer wish to serve the evil one, my passions, or sin. O Jesus, reign over this poor heart and make it yours forever. *R*/

Day 5

I gaze upon you, O most sweet redeemer, dressed in a mantle of purple. It is your royal attire. How it speaks to me of that blood which you shed solely for me. Grant, O Child Jesus, that I may respond to your great sacrifice, and not refuse when you offer me some difficulty to suffer with you and for you. *R*/

Day 6

O most lovable Child, in contemplating that you sustain the world, my heart fills with joy that I am amongst the beings that you sustain. You look on me, uphold me and guard me as your own granting me what I need for this life. *R/*

Day 7

On your breast, O Child Jesus, shines a cross. It is a standard of our redemption. I thank you I also have my cross, but, although light, it often weighs me down. Help me to bear it and may the carrying of it be fruitful. *R/*

Day 8

Together with the cross, I see on your breast, O Child Jesus, a little golden heart. It is the image of your heart, which is truly golden on account of its infinite tenderness. Continue to pour out your love on me, O Jesus, and teach me always to respond. *R/*

Day 9

How many blessings, O Little Child has your hand poured out on those who honour and call upon you. Bless me also, O Child Jesus, and help me in my necessities. I beg you, grant what I now desire. *R/*

Litanies

(For private devotion)

Litany of the Miraculous Infant of Prague

Lord have mercy.

Christ have mercy. Lord have mercy.

Christ hear us.

Christ graciously hear us.

Deliver us, O Jesus.

We beseech Thee hear us.

God the Father of heaven, *R/ Have mercy on us.*

God the Son, Redeemer of the world, *R/*

God the Holy Spirit *R/*

O Miraculous Infant Jesus, *R/*

Infant Jesus, true God and Lord, *R/*

Infant Jesus, whose omnipotence is manifested
    in a wonderful manner, *R/*

Infant Jesus, whose wisdom searches our hearts *R/*,

Infant Jesus, whose goodness continually inclines
    to aid us, *R/*

Infant Jesus, whose providence leads us to our last end
    and destiny, *R/*

Infant Jesus, whose truth enlightens the darkness of
 our hearts, *R/*
Infant Jesus, whose generosity enriches our poverty *R/*
Infant Jesus, whose friendship consoles the afflicted, *R/*
Infant Jesus, whose mercy forgives our sins, *R/*
Infant Jesus, whose strength invigorates us, *R/*
Infant Jesus, whose power turns away all evils, *R/*
Infant Jesus, whose justice deters us from sin, *R/*
Infant Jesus, whose power conquers hell, *R/*
Infant Jesus, whose lovely countenance attracts
 our hearts, *R/*
Infant Jesus, whose greatness holds the universe in
 its hand, *R/*
Infant Jesus, whose love-inflamed heart kindles
 our cold hearts, *R/*
Infant Jesus, whose miraculous hand raised in
benediction fills us with all blessings, *R/*
Infant Jesus, whose sweet and holy name rejoices
 the hearts of the faithful, *R/*
Infant Jesus, whose glory fills the whole world, *R/*

Be merciful, spare us, O Jesus.
Be merciful, graciously hear us, O Jesus.

From all evil, *R/ Deliver us, O Jesus*
From all sin, *R/*
From all distrust of thy infinite goodness, *R/*

From all distrust of thy infinite goodness
and miracles, *R/*
From all lukewarmness in thy veneration, *R/*
From trials and misfortunes, *R/*

Through the mysteries of thy holy childhood,
R/ We beseech thee, hear us
Through the intercession of Mary, thy Mother,
and Joseph, thy foster father, *R/*
That thou wouldst pardon us, *R/*
That thou wouldst bring us to true repentance, *R/*
That thou wouldst preserve and increase in us love
and devotion to thy sacred infancy, *R/*
That thou wouldst never withdraw thy miraculous
hand from us, *R/*
That thou wouldst keep us mindful of thy
numberless benefits, *R/*
That thou wouldst inflame us more and more
with love for thy Sacred Heart, *R/*
That thou wouldst graciously deign to hear all
who call upon thee with confidence, *R/*
That thou wouldst preserve our country in peace, *R/*
That thou wouldst free us from all evils, *R/*
That thou wouldst give eternal life to all who
act generously toward thee, *R/*
That thou wouldst pronounce a merciful sentence
on us at the judgement, *R/*

That thou wouldst in thy miraculous image
   remain our consoling refuge, *R/*
Jesus, Son of God and of Mary, *R/*

Lamb of God, who takes away the sins of the world,
spare us, O Jesus.
Lamb of God, who takes away the sins of the world,
graciously hear us, O Jesus.
Lamb of God, who takes away the sins of the world,
have mercy on us, O Jesus.

O Miraculous Infant Jesus, kneeling before thy sacred
image, we beseech thee to cast a merciful look on our
troubled hearts. Let thy tender heart, so inclined to pity,
grant us that grace which we ardently implore. Take from
us all affliction and despair, all the trials and misfortunes
with which we are burdened. For thy sacred infancy's sake,
hear our prayers and send us consolation and aid, that
we may praise thee, with the Father and the Holy Spirit,
forever and ever. Amen.

Litany of the Holy Childhood of Jesus

Lord, have mercy on us. Christ, have mercy on us. Lord,
have mercy on us.

   Christ, hear us. Christ, graciously hear us.
   God the Father, *R/ Have mercy on us.*
   God the Son, Redeemer of the world, *R/*

God the Holy Spirit, *R/*

Holy Trinity, One God, *R/*

O Divine Infant Jesus, sent to earth from Heaven, *R/*

O Divine Infant Jesus, born of Mary in Bethlehem, *R/*

O Divine Infant Jesus, wrapped in swaddling clothes, *R/*

O Divine Infant Jesus, placed in the crib, *R/*

O Divine Infant Jesus, praised by the angels, *R/*

O Divine Infant Jesus, adored by the shepherds, *R/*

O Divine Infant Jesus, proclaimed as Saviour, *R/*

O Divine Infant Jesus, announced by the star, *R/*

O Divine Infant Jesus, worshipped by the Magi, *R/*

O Divine Infant Jesus, presented in the temple, *R/*

O Divine Infant Jesus, embraced by Simeon, *R/*

O Divine Infant Jesus, revealed in the temple by Anna, *R/*

O Divine Infant Jesus, persecuted by King Herod, *R/*

O Divine Infant Jesus, fleeing into the exile of Eypt *R/*

O Divine Infant Jesus, crowning with martyrdom
the infants of Bethlehem, *R/*

O Divine Infant Jesus, rejoicing the heart of Mary
with your first words, *R/*

O Divine Infant Jesus, learning to take your first steps
in exile, *R/*

O Divine Infant Jesus, returning from Egypt
to be brought up in Nazareth, *R/*

O Divine Infant Jesus, example of obedience, *R/*

O Divine Infant Jesus, brought to the temple
at the age of twelve, *R/*

O Divine Infant Jesus, lost by Mary
    and Joseph on their return home, *R/*
O Divine Infant Jesus, sought for three days
    with great sorrow, *R/*
O Divine Infant Jesus, found with great delight, *R/*

Be merciful, O Jesus. Be merciful, hear us, O Jesus.

From all evil, *R/ Deliver us, O Jesus.*
From all sin, *R/*
From misconduct in the Church, *R/*
From quarrels and anger, *R/*
From lies and stealing, *R/*
From evil talk and bad example, *R/*
From bad habits, *R/*
By your Incarnation, *R/*
By your birth, *R/*
By your poverty, *R/*
By your persecution and suffering, *R/*
Through the intercession of your Mother, *R/*
Through the intercession of your foster father, *R/*
Through the intercession of the Holy Innocents, *R/*
Through the intercession of all the angels and saints, *R/*

We, your sinful children, beseech you to hear us.
Hear our prayer for the salvation of unbelievers,
R/ We beseech you to hear us.
With pity, *R/*
That you would look kindly upon our small gifts, *R/*

That you would number the men of God
    among the saints, *R/*

That you would bless their apostolic works, *R/*

That we may be zealous in preaching the gospel, *R/*

That we may keep our baptismal promises, *R/*

That we may rejoice to be children of our Father
    in heaven, *R/*

That we may pray as Christian children,
    freely and devoutly, *R/*

That we may grow in wisdom and virtue as we grow
    in years, *R/*

That we may never make an unworthy confession, *R/*

That we may receive Holy Communion with sincerity, *R/*

That you will inspire in us great love and devotion
    for your Mother, *R/*

That you will enlighten our pastors
    and give them strength, *R/*

That you will repay our benefactors with eternal gifts, *R/*

That you will have mercy on our enemies, *R/*

That you will have mercy on the souls in purgatory, *R/*

Lamb of God, who takes away the sins of the world,
spare us, O Lord.

Lamb of God, who takes away the sins of the world,
hear our prayer, O Lord.

Lamb of God, who takes away the sins of the world,
have mercy on us, O Lord.

V. Christ, hear us.

R. Christ, graciously hear us.

Our Father

Let us pray: Heavenly Father, who for the infant Jesus's sake adopted us as children and as heirs of heaven, look kindly upon children not of the faith and grant that they may share in our unearned and priceless fortune. We ask this through the Infant Jesus. Amen.

The Litany of the Infant Jesus

Lord have mercy. Christ, have mercy. Lord have mercy, Infant Jesus, hear us.

Infant Jesus, graciously hear us.

God the Father, *R/ Have mercy on us.*
God the Son, Redeemer of the world, *R/*
God the Holy Spirit, *R/*
Holy Trinity, One God, *R/*

Infant Jesus, true God, *R/*
Infant, Son of the Living God, *R/*
Infant, Son of the Virgin Mary, *R/*
Infant, begotten before the morning star, *R/*
Infant, Word made flesh, *R/*
Infant, wisdom of thy Father, *R/*
Infant, purity of thy Mother, *R/*
Infant, only Son of thy Father, *R/*

Infant, First-Born of thy Mother, *R/*
Infant, image of thy Father, *R/*
Infant, creator of thy Mother, *R/*
Infant, splendour of thy Father, *R/*
Infant, honour of thy Mother, *R/*
Infant, equal to thy Father, *R/*
Infant, subject to thy Mother, *R/*
Infant, joy of thy Father, *R/*
Infant, riches of thy Mother, *R/*
Infant, gift of thy Father, *R/*
Infant, offering of thy Mother, *R/*
Infant, precious fruit of a Virgin, *R/*
Infant, creator of man, *R/*
Infant, power of God, *R/*
Infant, our God, *R/*
Infant, our Brother, *R/*
Infant, perfect Man from thy conception, *R/*
Infant, ancient in wisdom from thy childhood, *R/*
Infant, Father of ages, *R/*
Infant, ancient of days, *R/*
Infant, giving life, and nourished at the breast, *R/*
Infant, eternal Word, *R/*
Infant, weeping in the crib, *R/*
Infant, thundering in heaven, *R/*
Infant, terror of hell, *R/*
Infant, joy of paradise, *R/*
Infant, dreaded by tyrants, *R/*

Infant, desired by the Magi, *R/*
Infant, exiled from thy people, *R/*
Infant, King in exile, *R/*
Infant, destroyer of idols, *R/*
Infant, vindicator of the glory of God, *R/*
Infant, strong in weakness, *R/*
Infant, powerful in abasement, *R/*
Infant, treasure of Grace, *R/*
Infant, fountain of Love, *R/*
Infant, author of the blessings of Heaven, *R/*
Infant, repairer of the evils of earth, *R/*
Infant, head of the Angels, *R/*
Infant, stem of the Patriarchs, *R/*
Infant, Word of the Prophets, *R/*
Infant, expectation of nations, *R/*
Infant, joy of the shepherds, *R/*
Infant, light of the Magi, *R/*
Infant, salvation of children, *R/*
Infant, hope of the just, *R/*
Infant, teacher of Doctors, *R/*
Infant, first-fruits of the Saints, *R/*
Spare us, O Infant Jesus, be merciful.

From the bondage of the children of Adam,
R/ Infant Jesus, deliver us.
From the slavery of the devil, *R/*
From the corruption of the world, *R/*

From the lusts of the flesh, *R/*
From pride, *R/*
From the blindness of mind, *R/*
From the perversity of will, *R/*
From our sins, *R/*
Through thy pure conception, *R/*
Through thy humble birth, *R/*
Through thy tears, *R/*
Through thy devout presentation, *R/*
Through thy holy life, *R/*
Through thy poverty, *R/*
Through thy sorrows, *R/*

Let us pray: O Lord Jesus, who allow the greatness of thine incarnate divinity and most sacred humanity to be born in time, to become a little child, and to suffer bitter death, grant that we may acknowledge infinite wisdom in the silence of a child, power in weakness, majesty in abasement, so that adoring thy humility and littleness on earth we may contemplate thy glories in heaven. Amen.

Prayer to the Santo Bambino di Aracoeli

Divine Child,
In my difficulties: help me
From the enemies of my soul: save me
In my errors: enlighten me
In my doubts and pains: comfort me

In my solitudes: be with me
In my infirmities: invigorate me
When others despise me: encourage me
In temptations: defend me
In difficult hours: strengthen me
With your Sacred Heart: love me
With your immense power: protect me
And, into your arms, when I die: receive me.
Amen.

Prayer to El Niño de Atocha

All-knowing Child of Atocha, protector of all men, protection of the weak, divine doctor of any illness; most powerful Child, I greet you, I praise you today and I offer you these three Our Fathers, and Hail Marys, with a Glory Be to the Father in memory of the journey that you made to Bethlehem incarnate in the pure womb of your most beloved other.

Our Father x3; Hail Mary x3; Glory Be.

I ask you to grant my request, which I submit in union with the choirs of cherubim and seraphim, adorned with the most perfect wisdom, because, precious Child of Atocha, I know that I will not be disappointed by you and I will obtain a good death in order to accompany you into glory. Amen.

Prayer to Le Petit Roi de Grâce

Memorare of the Infant Jesus

Remember, sweet Child Jesus, that you said to Venerable Margaret of the Most Blessed Sacrament, and through her, to all your devotees, these consoling words: "Ask for all your needs through the merits of my infancy and nothing will be denied you". Full of trust in you, who are truth itself, I present my prayer.

Give me the grace to lead an authentic Christian life; to obtain a happy eternity. By the infinite merits of your incarnation and childhood, grant my prayer (*here state the requested grace*). I commit myself to you, omnipotent Child, confident that you will heed my plea and will fortify me in hope. Amen.

Addresses

Infant of Prague

Klášter Pražského Jezulátka
Karmelitská 9,
118 00 Prague 1 - Malá Strana
Czech Republic
www.pragjesu.info

Little King of Grace

Monastère du Petit Roi de Grâce
14 rue de Chorey
21200 Beaune
France

Santo Bambino di Aracoeli

Santa Maria Aracoeli
Scala dell'Arce Capitolina, 12
00186 Rome
Italy